D0121751

THE
STRANGEST

Betty Shamieh

BROADWAY PLAY PUBLISHING INC
New York
www.broadwayplaypub.com
info@broadwayplaypub.com

Cover photo by Hunter Canning

First edition: June 2018
I S B N: 978-0-88145-786-5

Book design: Marie Donovan
Page make-up: Adobe InDesign
Typeface: Palatino

THE STRANGEST was first produced by The Semitic Root at the Fourth Street Theatre, opening on 15 March 2017. The cast and creative contributors were:

NADER .... Juri Henley-Cohn
NOUNU .... Louis Sallan
NEMO.. Andrew Guilarte
UMM .... Jacqueline Antaramian
ABU ....Alok Tewari
LAYALI... Roxanna Hope Radja
GUN .... Brendan Titley

Director..May Adrales
Creative producer................................... Allison Bressi
Scenic design...............................Daniel Zimmerman
Lighting design ....Aaron Porter
Costume design.............................. Becky Bodurtha
Original music & sound design...........Nathan A Roberts &
                                        Charles Coes
Executive producer ....Paradox Productions
Co-producer ....Five Ohm Productions
General manager...................................... Kaitlin Boland
Production stage manager ....Julia Celentano
Production manager ....Libby Jensen
Props master .... Theresa Pierce
Fight director .... Lisa Kopitsky
Dramaturg ....Katie Premus
Press representative ....Sin Gogolak
Technical director... Jeremiah Fox

CHARACTERS & SETTING

NADER, *male, twenties*
NOUNU, *male, twenties*
NEMO, *male, twenties*
UMM, *female, early forties*
ABU, *male, late forties*
LAYALI, *female, twenties*
GUN, *male, forties*

The actor playing GUN *should wear a very small pair of khaki shorts. On his head, he wears a large protruding piece of metal shaped to look like the barrel of a handgun. His speech is never naturalistic. He only says one word, "bang", throughout the entire play. The female characters treat him normally and react to him as if he is speaking the dialogue indicated in parentheses. He says the word "bang" in the place of each syllable of each word of the dialogue in parentheses, so that the scenes with him have the cadence of ordinary conversation.*

Setting: Algiers
Time: 1940s

NOTE

Midway through Albert Camus's novel *The Stranger*, an unnamed Arab is killed. This play is inspired by that unknown character. The play has two modes and the lighting should reflect the shifts between them. The first is the story of Umm, a female storyteller trying to integrate the all-male coffeehouses of Algeria. The second is the story that she tells. Umm will move back and forth between these two worlds seamlessly.

For Hany

Scene 1

UMM: Bet on me, men of Algeria! Bet on me! *(Pause)*
What? Silence. Come on. I have got pedigree. If
storytelling was a race and storytellers were racehorses,
I would be a winning bet. I am the daughter of the best
Storyteller in Algeria. The only man who ever beat my
father at the coffeehouse storytelling competition was
my husband and he only beat him once.
Maybe that's why you're just pretending to ignore
me instead of dragging me out like the last girl who
dared to enter here when a storytelling competition
was taking place. That girl had pedigree too. She
fought the French alongside you, brought the French
empire to its knees. Now you want to tell her that the
women's place is in the home. Good luck with that.
Do you really think you're going to keep a woman like
her, a killer, out of places like here, the Parliament, or
anywhere she wants to be for very long?
Waiters! Fill the cups of these men. I'll wait. They're
just about to take their bets on me. No? They're not
really going to refuse to bet on me because I'm a
woman, right? Or is because you don't have enough
information about the story I intend to tell that you
wait?
There will be intrigue in my tale. A murder mystery.
But, I should come clean. There will be no appearances
of genies or magic lamps. Just the annihilation of a son
of Algeria by a Frenchman for no reason. I will show
you three young men. You won't know which son of

Algeria would be shot until the end of the story. No magic carpets in the story either. Just an assassination of a child I bore and the French man who shot him down will feel nothing before, during, or after. Strange, isn't it?

I know it is more customary here, in the coffeehouse competitions, to tell tales from the Arabian Nights. But, times are changing. So, I will tell you a story about my family. The story I tell will be placed before the Battle of Algiers, in a time when no one could conceive that the French would ever go, not even most of us.

Shall I introduce my characters?

The sons of Algeria, sons of a woman like me.

My Nader, my Nounu, my Nemo.

(Lights up on each of them as she mentions them by name. They are in the 3 "monkey" see no evil, hear no evil, speak no evil positions.)

NADER: Your genius

NOUNU: Your shoemaker

NEMO: And your thief.

UMM: As different as night is to day, day is to dusk, dusk is to dawn.

Which will the Frenchman kill?

NADER: The good Arab?

NOUNU: The harmless Arab?

NEMO: The bad Arab?

(Lights up on ABU. He speaks with difficulty.)

ABU: Your best weapon is your ability to think.

UMM: *(To ABU)* It's not your turn yet.

(Lights down on ABU)

UMM: There is a babe in my tale.
Oh, yes!

What's a tale of murder and intrigue without a babe?
She's my husband's niece, Layali. I raised her.
I should have known it would end badly when Layali
brought a gun to dinner and introduced it as her fiancé.
See no evil, hear no evil, speak no evil are before you.
Let me introduce a fourth monkey, "fuck no evil".

(Lights up on LAYALI. *She is covering her privates [as if she were the "have sex with no evil" monkey].)*

LAYALI: Fair France,
send us your convicts,
your underemployed,
your underemployable,
your orphans,
your perverts,
your criminals,
and your beggars.
And I'll try my damnedest to marry one of them.

UMM: Why have I presented them as monkeys? Is it because the French called us that?

ABU: The French are not our enemy.

UMM: Did the murderer who shot down a beautiful son of Algeria for no reason do so because he thought the Arab wasn't worth more than a monkey? No, I tell you! No! If you *can* feel, you *do* feel something when you kill an animal. But, the French man who gunned my son down felt nothing.

ABU: The French—

UMM: *(To* ABU) If you don't shut up, Abu, I'm going to grind some glass into your hummus and watch you die slowly.
Excuse us.
Where was I?
Ah, yes!
There is the smoking gun.

The French would call him a Blackfoot.
Pied-noir.
That's what they called Frenchmen who are born in
Africa,
as if being born on our continent made part of you turn
black.
He introduced himself by some French name.
But, we called him Gun.
What's a good tale about murder without a smoking
gun?

(*Lights up on* GUN. *He is smoking. He waves. His manner
is extremely friendly.*)

GUN: Bang. (*Hello!*)

(ABU *steps forward.*)

UMM: Yes, it's finally time I introduced Abu.
This is how he sounds after he gave the speech that
would save the lives of half the men of our village.

ABU: (*Speaking with difficulty*) To be defenseless is not
the same thing as being defeated.

UMM: But you should have heard him before.

Don't you dare laugh at him, you young men in the
audience!
He used to be like you are now.
Magnificent.
Now, he's reduced to repeating the one speech that
saved half the lives of the men in this village when
the French came to massacre us. His eloquence is the
reason why many of you had fathers to fuck mothers to
make you. He saved so many except the one brother he
would have given anything to save.

LAYALI: My father!

UMM: He would keep replaying that speech over and over in his head.
Mock him not, young men of Algeria!
When you are his age, you will replay your shining moments too.
I bet they will not be as brilliant as his.
I bet the day you will go on reliving at the end of your days will not end in anything as glorious as saving half the men of your village.
Just like you will not have the eloquence he had before that day either.
He used to sound like this.

ABU: *(Speaking eloquently and slightly seductively)* Listen, my young bride. Stop crying. I'm not going to touch you. I promise. Just listen to me first for one moment. I have to tell you a story.

UMM: Just listen, he said.

ABU: After I am through with my story, you can go back to your crying and I promise you can tap back into the same well of tears. You lose nothing by giving me a moment of your time. You need to know how long I have been dreaming of you. Not any young pretty bride. You. This is our wedding night, so you must not be afraid of me. I will tell you how I won your hand and, if you take my hand after I tell you the story, I will know you are ready. If you do not, I will wait for you. I will lie by your side and not touch you until you take me by the hand. Then, I will know you are ready to let me love you. No, not ready. Eager.

UMM: 'Fat chance,' I thought to myself. 'I'll never willingly take your hairy hand.' I spit on his face, which is something I had never done before, but he deserved it. He had no right to scare me. He picked up the spit that landed on his cheek and put it in his mouth. 'My parents married me to a monster,' I thought. Spit was dirty and he took my spit into his mouth as if it was something sweet.

ABU: Yes, pretty wife, I saw you and thought you were the loveliest thing I could ever imagine. I was a boy then. I thought to myself, 'When I grow up, I want to marry her. How am I ever going to get her as my wife?' Her father is the famous Storyteller. Rich too. But, I put it in my head that I would have you and looked for my way. I knew the answer lay in beating your father at his own game. Storytelling. I would go a storytelling coffeehouse competition and beat him. But how? I had never told a story in public before. Then, an idea struck me. I knew a way to win. So, when the next competition came, I stood up and said, "Storyteller! Master of the Auditory Art! With all due respect, Sir, I would like to challenge you to a linguistic duel."

NADAR & NOUNU & NEMO: No one will bet on you, Boy.

UMM: Said my father. Not wanting to waste his time or embarrass the boy, who clearly had no chance of winning.

ABU: I told your father, "I'll bet on myself! If I lose, I'll work in your olive orchard for a year. If I win, you will give me the hand of one of your seven daughters in marriage and you will let me choose which will be my wife." Your father chose a little known tale from the Arabian Nights, the fable of Zumurrad. He enchanted the audience with this story of how a woman disguised herself as a man and became a great sultan, guiding her kingdom to prosperity. Sooner than I wanted it to be, it was my turn. I chose a better known tale, Ali Baba and the Forty Thieves. My voice rang out clearly, but I could not stop my legs from shaking. Nor could I keep the rudiments of my story in my head. I forgot the key element of the story, how Ali Baba overheard the thieves say "Open Sesame", magic words that opened a door to a secret cave where they kept their stolen treasures. This was an audience who had heard this story a thousand times before. I had to start again and, pretty bride, a few of the men in the audience began shouting for me to give it up, but your father said

NADAR & NOUNU & NEMO: No! Let the boy finish.

ABU: Then, I pulled out my secret weapon, the twist I planned all along. I told that crowd, 'When Ali Baba opened the door to the cave by saying the words "Open Sesame", he saw it was filled with riches beyond his delight.' But instead of describing the rubies and diamonds and pearls that the thieves had stored there, I said that the cave was filled with vineyards, orchards, citrus groves, coastal lands with breathtaking views of the sea. I said the cave of thieves was filled with fields of winter wheat, cotton, and barley. There were mines of iron and zinc in this magic cave. No one knew what to make of it, except your father who smiled broadly. For he knew what riches I was naming and where my story was going. Now, the story always had been Ali Baba and the Forty Thieves. Full stop. Forty Anonymous Thieves. But, in my version of the story, the thieves had names. I said the first thief was the king of thieves. That first thief's name was Charles X, an unpopular king who invaded a land far away to shore up support for his disastrous and despised reign. The second thief was Jules de Polignac, who justified eradicating people in their own land by calling its inhabitants "a nest of pirates." The third thief was Pere Bugeaud, a soldier who masterminded a new idea he called "scorched earth warfare", where families who hid from the fighting in the caves would be trapped and suffocated. And so on. I went down the line, counting off the forty thieves and giving them French names. Soon, the

men in the audience chimed in. They began to shout
the names of their torturers, names of men they have
never uttered aloud before, but whose lives – like the
lives of all torturers and their victims – would always
be inextricably linked, because they would forever see
each other's faces in their dreams. When I got to the
fortieth name, everyone cheered and picked me up
on their shoulders. Your father had to agree that the
crowd chose me as the winner.

Though you had older sisters who were considered
beauties, especially the eldest who was fair-haired and
green-eyed like your Turkish mother, I chose perfect
little you. And when I was told you were too young to
marry, I insisted I would wait for you until you were
old enough and I did. Why? Sweet bride, I fell in love
with you the night that a band of French hooligans
came to harass us and people from different villages
ran up into the mountains. I would never have married
a girl outside my clan if that night hadn't happened,
if the French had not driven us from our homes. It's
funny that nothing in our lives is untouched by them.
Sweet bride, do you remember that night? You were
only seven or so. All of the women—and many of the
men—cried as they drove us up the mountain. My
sister was only three. She had wet herself and was
crying uncontrollably. Nothing could stop her. The
crowd began to give the girl and my parents – who
were trying desperately to quiet her—murderous
looks. No one had any food or anything to give her
that might make her calm again, except you. You had
a doll, a doll you clearly loved so much you wouldn't
run out of your home without it. I could see you, just
a child yourself. I saw you look at my sister and look
at the doll and I watched you decide to give it to her.
It made her stop crying for a moment, the surprise of
suddenly having a doll.

I decided then and there that I wanted to marry you
and only you. I would have to dream up a way to have
you and I did. The French had entered our nightmares
from the moment they landed on our land a hundred
years ago. It was only a matter of time before they
entered our stories. So, I'm going to sleep on this side
of the bed and won't touch you if you don't take my
hand, pretty bride. I may seem terrifying to you, but
you're pretty terrifying to me. I've never been alone
with anyone else in a bed either. I will wait as long
as it takes for you to touch me first. Because I don't
want you to be ready to do with me what husbands
and wives do, I want you to be eager. I could never do
something that would scare such a tender-hearted girl.
My sister died soon after, and she died clutching the
doll you gave her. Do you remember that night, the
night I fell in love with you?

UMM: I do. But I didn't bring a doll. It was my cousin,
Tamara, who gave hers to your sister. You married the
wrong girl. *(Pause)* Just kidding.

(UMM *tentatively takes* ABU *by the hand. They both sigh
deeply.)*

UMM: Would you have really waited for me to touch
you first?

ABU: Of course. For ten minutes.

UMM: That is what Abu, the father of the son who will
be shot down by a Frenchman, sounded like when he
was young. But, now he sounds like this...

ABU: *(Having difficulty speaking and sounding much older)*
The French are not our enemy

UMM: Now, he sounds like a man who knows that
eloquence can't win you everything.
So, there! I have introduced my characters to you.

Now, we're ready to hear which son of mine was killed
and how.
Wait! I forgot.
I myself will play a minor role in this tale of murder.
It's my fault he died.
Because it is always a mother's fault when a child dies,
if you don't believe me,
it's because you're not a mother who lost her child.
What do you need to know about me?
You know a lot already, right?
I'm the dead boy's mother.
I am the daughter of the best Storyteller in Algeria and
the wife of the only man who ever beat him.

(The lights shift to reflect that the prologue is over.)

UMM: It all began the night that Layali brought a gun
to our house and introduced it as her fiancé.

(The lights shift back to prologue setting.)

UMM: No, that's not right. It began earlier than that.
It began when, against my better judgment, I took in
my husband's niece after her father was shot. I should
not have taken the girl and her brother in when their
mother left them on my doorstep. Layali was causing
havoc in my house way before that fateful day and,
though no one here has bet on me, I will tell you a
story.

(Lights down on UMM.)

Scene 2

(Lights up on LAYALI, NADER, NEMO, and NOUNU)

LAYALI: We have to.

NADER: No, *we* don't have to do anything, Layali.

LAYALI: I'll show you mine again.

NOUNU: I've already seen it.

LAYALI: Show me yours again right now. Do you realize what's going to happen to me? I'm going to start to bleed and then I'm going to get married. You can go to the whorehouse. You can even marry more than one wife, but I'm only going to see one man's privates. Do you realize how unfair that is?

NADER: You've already seen mine and all the boys in the neighborhood and you're only nine. I think you're doing pretty good for nine.

LAYALI: Don't try to act all adult on me.

NOUNU: Not going to do it again. It's not right.

NEMO: Last time, we got caught and you said it was my idea.

LAYALI: So? All your mom did was laugh and tell us not to do it anymore. I don't care. Let me see! I want to see! You're just mad because I have more hair. That means I'm more of an adult. Let me see if you've grown more hair.

NADER: No.

(Lights down on NADER*)*

NOUNU: No.

(Lights down on NOUNU*)*

LAYALI: I'm glad it's just you and me, Nemo. Come on. Let me see yours.

NEMO: It's wrong. You're not my wife.

LAYALI: I know but don't you want me to be? You're my cousin. You have first dibs on me. You do want to marry me, don't you? You said it at the mosque and everyone laughed. Say you want to marry me!

NEMO: I want to marry you.

LAYALI: I know. Nemo, if you want me to be your wife, I will be. We're going to be married when we are old enough. So, my privates are yours and yours are mine, and I want to see yours now.

NEMO: Okay.

LAYALI: Touch it.

NEMO: Okay.

(After they've revealed themselves to each other, NEMO touches her privates. A bright light shines as ABU enters into their space. He is menacing and grabs NEMO by the arm.)

ABU: Don't you touch her! I'll kill you!

NEMO: Dad! No!

(There is a sound of a bone cracking and a scream. Lights up on UMM.)

UMM: Kids will be kids. But, parents will be parents and my husband broke little Nemo's arm for touching his niece. If that wasn't warning enough that the girl was danger, I don't know what would have been.

(Lights up on LAYALI. She passes NOUNU on her way to the section of the stage where UMM is sitting.)

NOUNU: Hi! I made you a pair of shoes.

LAYALI: Nounu! We talked about this. Leather is way too expensive for you to make me new shoes. I don't need them.

NOUNU: High heels.

LAYALI: How high?

NOUNU: Five centimeters.

LAYALI: Beautiful. *(Pause)* I'll sell them to one of the mothers of my students.

NOUNU: I didn't make them for a mother of your students. I made them for you.

(*Lights up on* NEMO)

NEMO: (*He hands her pearls.*) How about this? You like that, don't you?

LAYALI: Are these real pearls?

NEMO: Yeah.

LAYALI: Where did you get them?

NEMO: Found them. Around Malika Abbass's neck.

LAYALI: You're a dirty thief and the police are going to get you.

NEMO: Everyone steals everything. Why does morality only apply to me? The French stole my grandfather's acre of olive trees.

LAYALI: Yes. But, you steal from Arabs, not French people. I won't take them.

NEMO: Why are you here?

LAYALI: I'm here to see your mother. Is she here?

NEMO: You're not here to see my mother. You're here to twitch your hips around me and to drive me crazy like you always do.

(NEMO *tries to kiss* LAYALI, *she pulls away.*)

NEMO: Forget it.

(*Lights down on* NEMO)

LAYALI: 'Forget it' is right.

(*Lights up on* NADER.)

LAYALI: Nader! Is your mom home?

NADER: Yes.

LAYALI: Okay, see you!

NADER: Wait! Are you in a hurry?

LAYALI: No.

NADER: Then stay a while. Want to see my painting?

LAYALI: I always want to see your painting. *(She sees the painting)* It's very...

NADER: It's abstract. I know you don't like abstract art.

LAYALI: I don't think people will buy such paintings, Nader.

NADER: I'm telling you that people like abstract paintings, paintings that evoke feelings.

LAYALI: French people, you mean. Fine. If you say so.

NADER: Have you thought about what we talked about?

LAYALI: Yes. And I'm still thinking about it.

NADER: What's your answer?

(Pause)

LAYALI: Abu-Murad came by after my class today.

NADER: Son of a bitch.

LAYALI: Why are you calling him names?

NADER: Why do you think? Don't tell me. He offered to hire you, right? As a maid?

LAYALI: As a tutor. You know I would never be a maid for anyone. He asked me if I would consider tutoring his kids full-time. He is embarrassed that his children don't speak proper French. It would be twice the salary.

NADER: You know he's asked every pretty girl in this town if she wants to work for him. They say he raped Fady's daughter and I believe it.

LAYALI: He won't try to fuck with me.

NADER: How do you know?

LAYALI: Because I know. Everyone from the town knows how my dad died. Even collaborators like Abu-Murad are afraid of the ghost of a hero.

NADER: I wouldn't count on that.

LAYALI: His wife is the biggest idiot you've ever met. She buys the dresses I make. I can get her and her friends to buy your paintings. Because I can speak French, they assume I'm smarter. I made hundreds of franks off of them.

NADER: You didn't make that kind of money selling dresses.

LAYALI: Nader, what do you think I did to get that money?

(Pause)

NADER: I think you had a boyfriend.

LAYALI: And you didn't try to stop me?

NADER: How could I stop you? I'm your cousin. Not your jailer.

LAYALI: How very enlightened of you! How very French of you! I did sell those dresses and the reason those women paid those prices for them is because I made French labels that looked like designer labels. I told them I had a hook-up on hot goods from France. That is how we can sell your paintings.

NADER: By sewing Chanel to them?

LAYALI: Not Chanel. But, sign your paintings with another French name and I can sell them.

NADER: I'm not just trying to sell paintings.

LAYALI: What? Then what are you trying to do?

NADER: The names of our streets have French signs on them. The constitution that says we are subjects, not citizens of our own country, is written in French.

I want to be a major artist. I don't want to sell under another name. I want to glorify my own. Not just for my sake, but for the sake of all Algeria.

LAYALI: We have enough men in our family who are only good at talking big and accomplishing nothing.

NADER: I'm going to do more than talk big. I will sell paintings under my own name and a lot of them. Jean is going to introduce me to all the right people. Jean knows my worth. He says I am...

LAYALI: Am what?

NADER: I shouldn't say it about myself. But, he says I am brilliant.

LAYALI: Jean is trying to fuck you.

NADER: I know. But, can't both things be true? Can't he think I am brilliant and be trying to fuck me?

LAYALI: Both things *can* be true. But, I wouldn't assume they are. I wouldn't bet my life on it. Nothing clouds an artistic assessment like an erection. Has he asked you to fuck him?

NADER: No. *(Pause)* He just asks me if I was sure I am not curious about men. Almost every time I see him.

LAYALI: And?

NADER: And he occasionally offers me blowjobs.

LAYALI: Wow! It's rich that he offers you the one thing...

NADER: The one thing...what?

LAYALI: The one thing I can feel you thinking about when you look at my mouth.

NADER: What are you talking about?

LAYALI: I can tell. When I speak, you look at my mouth. I probably should wear a veil that covers my face around you, Cousin. It's the only way to be sure to get a man to look you in the eye. Let's play French. *(Speaking with a French accent)* Hello, Cousin Jacques!

NADER: Layali, I'm sick of that game. I deserve an answer.

LAYALI: *(French accent)* Hello, Cousin Jacques!

NADER: Will you or won't you marry me, Layali? We're not so young anymore.

LAYALI: *(Dropping the accent)* If you play French with me, I'll give you a kiss.

NADER: On the mouth?

LAYALI: See. I knew you were obsessed with my mouth. Fine. On the mouth. *(French accent)* Hello, Cousin Jacques!

NADER: *(Reluctantly speaking with a French accent)* Hello, Cousin Jacqueline!

LAYALI: *(French accent)* Have you eaten your croissant, Jacques?

NADER: *(French accent)* Oui, Jacqueline.

LAYALI: *(French accent)* So, Jacques, you are a great artist, no? A genius! That is what your friend Jean calls you, even when you're not there.

NADER: *(Dropping the accent)* You've met Jean. How?

LAYALI: *(French accent)* A cultured French girl makes it her business to know everyone, especially famous writers like Jean Genet. I want to speak of your work, Jacques. I need to know if you would be willing to do whatever it takes to sell more of it. Let's imagine being a French artist is passé. You can fetch a higher price for your work if you put an Arab name on it.

NADER: *(French accent)* Cousin Jacqueline, my work is brilliant. No one will believe that it was made by an Arab. A brilliant Arab, can you imagine? No!

Impossible, though we Frenchmen have tried to bring enlightenment to those Algerian savages. In our enlightened way, we have lightened them of their land, their livelihood, and their lives.

LAYALI: *(Dropping the French accent)* Stop, Nader! This is no fun.

NADER: Really? I was just getting into it.

LAYALI: French people would never talk this much about Arabs. We are like rats to them. The only thing to talk about when discussing rats is how to get rid of them, and that isn't a very long conversation at all.

NADER: You're right. This game sucks, Layali. Let's sneak into the orchard. I want my kiss.

LAYALI: It doesn't suck. We're just not doing it right. You have to deal with the French at salons. You want them to buy your paintings and respect your work. Don't lie. I know you do, especially this famous writer, Jean. He matters to you. So, you have to understand them, because this man, Jean, is one of them. No matter how much he talks about a world without nations where wealth is shared, he is still one of them. To be one of them is to not have to think about people of other races unless you choose to. What's that like? To go through life and never have to wonder what they will allow your kind to do or be or have or want? *(French accent)* Let's play the game right, Cousin Jacques.

NADER: *(French accent)* Fine, Cousin Jacqueline. Let's speak of something I know that a fine Frenchman like me would be concerned with. Marriage proposals. I cannot wait forever.

LAYALI: *(French accent)* Tell me more about your work.

NADER: *(French accent)* What is your answer, Cousin Jacqueline?

LAYALI: *(French accent)* When I speak of your work, it relates directly to your marriage proposal. They are two sides of the same coin. I am a fine French lady, Cousin Jacques. Therefore a man's work and his marriage proposal go together in my mind. I need to know if your paintings will sell and, Cousin Jacques, sell they must. Will they make you money? *(Dropping the French accent)* Enough to move your parents and me out of a one-room shack into an actual house? With a bathroom? With running water?

NADER: I don't know.

LAYALI: *(French accent)* Then, I don't know to your marriage proposal, Cousin Jacques.

NADER: I hate this game. I want my kiss.

LAYALI: Later. When we're alone.

NADER: We're alone when we go to the orchard.

LAYALI: I'm here to see your mother.

NADER: I knew I shouldn't have trusted you.

(Lights down on NADER. NEMO enters the scene.)

NEMO: I got a game for you, Cousin Jacqueline. It's called the-bend-the-prissy-whore-over-and-fuck-her-up-the-ass-game.

LAYALI: Shut up! I don't know why you get like this, Nemo!

NEMO: I get more points if the prissy bitch I bend over is a money-grubbing whore. You don't like that game, very much, do you? Huh, cousin Jacqueline?

LAYALI: I said, shut up, you stupid bastard.

NEMO: Thought you liked the game of playing French. Used to make me play it with you all the time, and that's not the only game either. My dad caught us playing doctor and you watched him break my arm without telling him that particular game was all your idea.

LAYALI: What did you expect me to do? He wouldn't have believed it if I told him the truth.

(NOUNU *enters.*)

NOUNU: You could have tried.

LAYALI: Oh, you! It wasn't my fault. Your father sprung so quickly.

NEMO: His precious niece! Feels bad about how your dad died so he breaks my arm if he thinks I'm treating you wrong. I wish he could see the truth about you. I know you're looking for a man with more money than anyone in your clan can provide.

NOUNU: There are worthy men in your own clan who want you.

NEMO: Better than worthy. Better than you deserve. I'll go and clap at your motherfucking wedding and I'll be smiling! Smiling. How often do you get to go to a wedding where you know exactly what the ass of the bride looks like as intimately as I know yours? You were nine when I saw your ass. That means I saw it at its best, Cousin Jacqueline. So, don't turn into a blushing flower now.

LAYALI: I'm not a blushing flower. And you're right. You'll have that experience. Seeing me marry a man with more money that you can ever make in a lifetime and, when that happens, you dirty bastard, don't think I'll give a second thought to what you are thinking on that day! (*She leaves.*)

NOUNU: Making her angry is not a good idea.

NEMO: You shouldn't give a fuck about her. No man should. She doesn't have anything I can't get at the whorehouse. She just comes here to get an ego boost.

To know there is someone always panting after her, even though she's not so young anymore.

NOUNU: No, she isn't. But, still beautiful.

NEMO: She is an adult woman of a marriageable age. Her brother was right to make her move in with him and his wife. She doesn't live here anymore. She shouldn't be hanging around here anymore. I'm going to jump her one of these day.

NOUNU: Don't be vulgar.

NEMO: Bitch! I saw her little pussy and I wish I hadn't. I can't get it out of my head.

NOUNU: It's hard not to want her.

(Lights up on NADER.)

NEMO: Want to listen to what she is going to speak about with Mama?

NADER: No, I'm not an eavesdropper. I should go to the salon.

NEMO: Forget the salon. Whorehouse. That's the place to be. Forget about her for a while. Or fuck a whore really hard and pretend it is her.

NADER: She's a cousin!

NEMO: That's why I'm fucking a whore and haven't jumped her. Yet. I could get her in the orchard somehow and cover her mouth.

NOUNU: That wouldn't be nice.

NEMO: Shut up!

NADER: No one is jumping anyone.

NEMO: We'll see about that.

NADER: And the pearls are going back. People are going to notice that they lose jewelry when they visit our family's shoe-shop.

NOUNU: It is bad for business. I want to hear what she is here to talk about with Mother, but I'm afraid we'll get caught.

NEMO: What's the big deal?

NADER: I guess there is no harm in listening.

(NADER, NEMO, *and* NOUNU *go to the part of the stage where they can hear* UMM *and* LAYALI *talking together.*)

Scene 3

(*Lights up on* UMM *and* LAYALI.)

UMM: Layali, hello!

LAYALI: How are you, Aunty?

UMM: The same.

LAYALI: Did you take your shot yet?

UMM: No, do you mind?

(LAYALI *takes out an insulin shot and give it to* UMM.)

UMM: You always are the most gentle.

LAYALI: It's nothing, Aunty.

UMM: Did you bring the postcard your friend Meriem sent?

LAYALI: No. I didn't.

UMM: It's not right of your friend to only send you one postcard the entire year she is in France.

LAYALI: Some papers are saying that the French government is working with the Germans, that they are rounding up Jews and sending them away to Germany.

UMM: Well, if Meriem is in Germany now, she could still write. You know I want to see the postcard she sent you.

LAYALI: I know. I'll bring it next time. *(Pause)* Aunty, I'm going to leave my job at the school. Abu-Murad asked for me to come and be a private French tutor to his daughter. He's doing well these days. The French appointed him "governor of tribal affairs."

UMM: Is that what we're calling the collaborators these days? You know his reputation.

LAYALI: Do you think I'm going to let a dirty old man take advantage of me?

UMM: Fady's daughter said he raped her.

LAYALI: Fady's daughter wasn't careful. That's not going to happen to me. I'm not the type of girl that gets raped. I've always felt that. That I am the type of woman who no one can touch.

UMM: Don't talk that way. It makes you sound, forgive me for saying it, ignorant. And it is tempting fate.

LAYALI: I don't talk like that with others. Just with you. I'll be making good money. I can help Nader with the cost of his art supplies.

UMM: That's kind of you.

LAYALI: It's not kind. It's payback. I owe this family so much, especially you.

UMM: Stop that.

LAYALI: You're more than a mother to me. The woman who gave birth to me is evil. She's unnatural.

UMM: Don't say that. Your mother's not a monster, Layali. Her new husband made her give you and your brother up. Many women would abandon their children for a man. If most do not, it's only because the right man has not asked in the right way.

LAYALI: You wouldn't leave a child for a man, would you?

(Pause)

UMM: I don't think so.

LAYALI: No, you wouldn't leave Nader for the entire world. I wish I could live here with you again. I hate living with my brother and his cow of a wife.

UMM: Layali, you don't lie to me, do you?

LAYALI: Why would you ask me that?

UMM: The medicine you get me costs a fortune. Nader said that you offered him hundreds of franks for art supplies. That's a lot more money than you could have gotten by selling dresses, Layali. How did you really make that money?

(Pause)

LAYALI: I let a Frenchman paint me.

UMM: Really?

LAYALI: Yes. The famous writer, Jean, who bought some of Nader's paintings, helped me. I asked him for a job and he found me one as a model for a painter. The painter is a man like Jean. They don't like girls. He just paints me and pays me a lot for it.

UMM: Layali, do you undress?

LAYALI: It's not sexual. You don't understand. He is interested in my breasts, but he doesn't desire them. It's very weird—to be looked at with interest and not desire.

UMM: Why work for Abu-Murad now? Stay at the school. Sister Marie said you might be Vice Principal one day. Aren't you supposed to talk to her about it?

LAYALI: I did and she said maybe. That means maybe in twenty years. Sister Marie is okay, but the rest of those bitchy nuns won't allow it. For our sake, the French open charitable schools for Algerian girls, but

they never manage to let us Algerians run them. It's
a miracle she convinced them to let me teach French.
After we spoke, I decided I need a change. Abu-Murad
has a son.

UMM: And?

LAYALI: I can get him to marry me.

(Pause)

UMM: You would marry outside your clan, when you
have perfectly good offers from good men.

LAYALI: I will obey you in anything you ask of me.

UMM: I would never ask you to do anything you don't
want to do.

LAYALI: I want a house, Aunty. I want a house so
badly, I cannot tell you how badly I want a house. I so
hate one-room shacks of corrugated iron.

UMM: Like this one?

LAYALI: Don't make me ashamed. If you want me to
marry Nader, just tell me.

UMM: Do you know why Abu-Murad's family has a
house?

LAYALI: They're rich.

UMM: We're all refugees.

LAYALI: I know, Aunty.

UMM: No, you don't! Don't tell me what you know!
Before we fled, I hid my gold jewelry under a loose tile
under my bed, because I wanted to keep it safe from
thieves. It was inconceivable to me that someone could
keep me away from my house forever.

LAYALI: Aunty, should I take the job or not?

UMM: You're taking this job strictly in the hopes of
being closer to young Murad, right?

LAYALI: Yes.

UMM: Then, you're taking it because you hope to marry the son of the one woman in our town who understood the French meant business, that they would never allow us to return. Abu-Murad's wife wore all her gold on her, so she was able to sell it. Most of us needed to borrow money from them to eat. When the French came looking for a collaborator to appoint as "tribal leader"—they looked for someone amongst us with something to lose. They found Abu-Murad. And his wife. The French assassinate anyone who questions Abu-Murad's authority, including the old Storyteller. Instead of my son, the grandson of that dear old Storyteller, you want to marry the son of that woman who knew which way the wind was blowing and now has a house.

(Pause)

LAYALI: Yes.

UMM: Then, I advise you to take the job.

LAYALI: I just need to know you won't be angry if I—

UMM: Refuse a marriage offer of a son of mine?

LAYALI: Like I said, I will do anything you want.

UMM: If you marry Murad, do you think he will be generous with you?

LAYALI: I know he will. Aunty, I will squeeze that dirty collaborator's family for every ounce I can get. I will always make sure you have the insulin shots you need, no matter what the price. Nader is going to get his art supplies. No one that you love is going to want for anything.

UMM: You're a good girl.

(Lights shift to NADER, NEMO, *and* NOUNU.*)*

NADER: This is so humiliating.

NOUNU: I can't believe it. My own mother is willing to sell a woman that she knows her son loves.

NEMO: They're both bitches.

NADER: Shut your mouth!

(NADER *goes to attack* NEMO. NEMO *takes out a knife.*)

NOUNU: This is awful.

NADER: Put the knife away. Or else.

NEMO: Or else what? Who you going to call? The French police?

NADER: Yes. You need help. Stealing compulsively. Pulling a knife on people. I lied about how I got those cuts last time, but I can't lie forever.

NEMO: You think the French are going to put me in a hospital?

NOUNU: It's just jail for every Algerian that they find.

NADER: If Layali marries the son of that collaborator, she's doing it so she can help me. Mom and she are doing this for me.

(NEMO *puts the knife away.*)

NEMO: You wish. Fuck off and die!

(*Lights down on* NEMO)

NADER: She wants to help me. She said she wants to help me.

NOUNU: She also said she wants a house.

Scene 4

(LAYALI, *visibly upset, walks past* GUN.)

GUN: Bang. (*Hello*)

LAYALI: Fuck you! Don't talk to me, you fucking dirty French motherfucker. Don't look at me. Don't even fucking think about me!

(GUN *makes a move towards her. His manner is friendly, unmenacing.* NADER *enters and* GUN *walks away.*)

NADER: Layali. Is that you?

LAYALI: Yes.

NADER: What are you doing in the French quarter?

LAYALI: Jean told me where to find you. I need to talk to you. I'm going crazy. I want to kill someone.

NADER: Who?

LAYALI: Abu-Murad.

NADER: Did that motherfucker touch you?

LAYALI: No. But, I want to kill him and his son. The whole family of fucking collaborators. Every Frenchman I see.

NADER: Whoa! Whoa! Stop yelling. Let's go. Do you want a cup of coffee?

LAYALI: Where? They won't serve us in the French quarter.

NADER: They will at Café Blanc. I go there with Jean.

LAYALI: But Jean's not here.

NADER: I promise they'll serve me there. I go alone sometimes. He told them to let me order on his tab.

LAYALI: I don't need to be kicked out of a French café right now. If I see an illiterate fucking waiter sneer at serving us, I'm liable to start spitting.

NADER: They'll serve us there. Besides, you're so light-skinned they probably won't notice you're not French. Come on.

Scene 5

(LAYALI *and* NADER *are seated at a café table.*)

LAYALI: "May I take your order, Mademoiselle?" Miss Blondie asks me as if it is the most normal thing in the world. A French bitch serving me. Can you imagine? I can't get over it. Let me make the bitch redo my coffee. This cup is cold.

NADER: Lower your voice, Layali.

LAYALI: Don't worry. This is nice. Isn't it?

NADER: To have a drink by the sea?

LAYALI: Not that. Though they were smart—the French—to take the beachfront land first. I just mean sitting here, you and I. It's nice. So many times we played acting "French" and this setting makes it more real.

NADER: Can you tell me what's wrong now? Did Abu-Murad touch you? Because I can tell your brother and we'll go to his house. He can't go around asking Arab women to work for him and then—

LAYALI: Abu-Murad didn't ask me to work for him.

NADER: What?

LAYALI: And I wasn't tutoring anyone. After Sister Marie told me the school would never promote me, I approached Abu-Murad and offered to be his maid.

NADER: A maid? You? After what he did to Fady's daughter?

LAYALI: I'm not like Fady's daughter. My father was a hero.

NADER: Abu-Murad is a traitor and he got my grandfather killed. Do you think your father's honor is something he would value?

LAYALI: I wanted to get into that house so badly.

NADER: Why?

LAYALI: I wanted to marry his only son. I was sure I could make him agree to marry me. He doesn't like women, you know. Jean told me that he fucked every Frenchman he could get his hands on. So, I went to the fool and offered myself as his wife. I told him, 'You need to find a wife. You need to have children. No woman who knows what you are will be a more understanding wife than I. Marry me and you will be free to do as you wish.' And he said no. And he insulted me. Called me names. That's why I told him that I would tell everyone that he sleeps with Frenchmen, that he takes it up the ass, unless he married me.

NADER: That's not a good plan, Layali. Trying to blackmail a man into marrying you. And it's not safe. He could have tried to silence you and he could get away with it.

LAYALI: Don't get all righteous on me. I didn't go there planning to say I would threaten him. It just came out. I'm very bad, Nader.

NADER: You're not bad. You're just misguided.

LAYALI: And now I can't go back to school. The nuns gave my job away to a new girl.

NADER: I can stop painting and go back to making shoes full time.

LAYALI: Nader, you hate making shoes.

NADER: If I go back full-time, we can sew French labels into the shoes and—

LAYALI: Just stop. You want to be a painter. You don't want me.

NADER: Don't tell me what I want.

LAYALI: I am going to tell you the truth because I love you, Cousin. I am just one woman. After you have had me for a while, you will want another. If we were married, we would eventually hate one another.

NADER: Layali, if you don't want to marry me, don't marry me. But, don't tell me how I will feel about you or anything else.

LAYALI: I don't have energy for this right now.

NADER: You're going to be the death of me.

LAYALI: You're not cutting yourself again.

NADER: That was an accident.

LAYALI: Nader, I can't worry about you right now. I don't have room in my head right now to worry about you. You have to take care of yourself. (Feigns French tone) Promise, Cousin Jacques.

NADER: I've never cut myself, Cousin Jacqueline.

LAYALI: Then, how did you get those scars?

NADER: I got in a fight.

LAYALI: With who?

NADER: I told you. A Frenchman.

LAYALI: (Dropping the accent) Promise me.

NADER: Promise me that you won't pose anymore for French painters. Or do anything rash. I'm worried about you. When you get like this, you're liable to do anything. I know what you're thinking about doing.

LAYALI: What?

NADER: Don't make me say it. If you let a French bastard paint you naked or do something else with you for money, it won't be worth it. You'll find another teaching job.

LAYALI: Will you ask Jean? He said he doesn't know anyone hiring a French tutor, but he would look harder if you asked.

NADER: If he said he doesn't know anyone, he doesn't know anyone.

LAYALI: Jean's a famous writer. I'm sure he can get me a job if you ask him. He talks like he cares so much about Arabs. Tell him instead of writing plays about Arabs, he can do something even better and help an actual Arab. Me.

NADER: I'm just always asking him for things – art supplies, connections, to buy my paintings. Maybe the nuns know someone who might be able to hire you.

LAYALI: The nuns won't help me. Not after the scene I made when Sister Marie made it clear they'd never promote an Arab girl.

NADER: What kind of scene?

LAYALI: Never mind. But, if you can get Jean to get me a job, I won't have to think about (*pause*) doing anything else.

NADER: I'll ask Jean.

LAYALI: How could I have been so stupid?

(LAYALI *cries on* NADER'*s shoulder and wraps her arms around him. He gets turned on, he tries to hide it, but can't stop himself from stroking her arms and back with increasing passion as she sobs.*)

LAYALI: Nader?

NADER: What?

LAYALI: Stop.

NADER: Okay.

Scene 6

(Lights up on UMM *and* LAYALI. LAYALI *is mopping the floor on her hands and knees. Lights up on* GUN. *He is sitting at a table, smoking and drinking as he watches* LAYALI *mop the floor.)*

UMM: But, the French writer that befriended Nader and that Layali counted on left Algeria, which meant she had to find her own job. As a maid. Cleaning a café like the one where a French waitress once served her coffee, a moment she would always savor. Which meant she had to walk through the French quarter, work in the French quarter, spend most of her waking hours in the French quarter.

(Lights down on UMM. GUN *approaches* LAYALI. *His mannerism is courteous and cheerful.)*

GUN: Bang. *(Hello)*

LAYALI: Can I help you?

GUN: Bang. *(Have you heard of the Miss Algiers contest?)*

LAYALI: I'm not interested in being in a beauty contest.

GUN: Bang. *(I have a friend who is a judge.)*

LAYALI: Do you think the only way I could win a beauty contest is if it was rigged? Is that how you flatter women?

GUN: Bang. *(No, no. I didn't mean that. Don't get angry.)*

LAYALI: I'm not angry. I was just kidding. I kid a lot. You're going to have to know that if…

GUN: Bang. *(If what?)*

LAYALI: If we're going to be friends.

Scene 7

(Lights up on LAYALI. *After a pause, lights upon* NADER.)

NADER: Layali, what is wrong?

LAYALI: Follow me into the orchard.

NADER: What do you want?

LAYALI: You know what I want. Don't make me say it. Come on, Nader. I'm ready for you..

NADER: Are you pregnant?

LAYALI: No, I'm a virgin. You scumbag! To ask me that!

NADER: Then, why the sudden eagerness to make love? Unless you had something to hide. I don't understand.

LAYALI: I am a free person. I want to know what sex is. I want my first time to be with you. And only you. I don't want to give it away to someone who won't appreciate me.

NADER: So, you'll be my wife?

LAYALI: I want my first time to be tender. Follow me, Nader.

NADER: Your first time? Only your first time?

LAYALI: Stop it. This is so unromantic. Just shut up with the questions.

NADER: So you'll be my wife?

LAYALI: I'm never going to be your wife, Nader. I'm not going to make you happy.

NADER: Don't say that.

LAYALI: Okay, you're not going to make me happy. But I want to fuck now. I can get someone else if you don't want to fuck me. Nader, come on. This is your chance.

NADER: Stay away from me.

(Lights down on NADER. *Lights up on* NOUNU. *He is putting his clothes on dejectedly.)*

NOUNU: I'm sorry, Layali.

LAYALI: Don't be. It's fine. We can try another night.

NOUNU: I let you down.

LAYALI: Shhh. That's okay. I think it's probably—I don't know—the cold.

NOUNU: When you came by the shoe shop today and asked me to meet you here, I got so excited. I couldn't stop myself from abusing myself. I shouldn't have let myself get so excited. I made you beautiful shoes. French high heels. I copied them from a design I saw.

LAYALI: Don't make anything for me. I don't deserve it. Nounu, I don't want this to mess with you head. What happened between us right now is normal. It's perfectly normal that it sometimes doesn't work between a man and a woman. Thank God that it is. God, if men could get it up every time they wanted, they'd be even bigger monsters than they already are.

NOUNU: I am not a monster.

LAYALI: I know. I'm not calling you a monster. If there is anyone who is a monster, it's me.

NOUNU: You're not a monster. You're the most beautiful thing in the world. Look, I want you to have the best shoes ever. I'll make any kind of design you want. Just show me and I'll make it.

LAYALI: I don't deserve anything from you.

NOUNU: I don't want your feet in French-made shoes. I want you to walk only in what I make. Okay?

LAYALI: Okay.

NOUNU: Good. Now, don't ask me to meet you in the orchard again.

(Lights down on NOUNU. *Lights up on* NEMO.*)*

NEMO: I couldn't believe my luck when you whispered in my ear that you wanted me to meet you in the orchard. What do you want, Bitch?

LAYALI: For you to fuck me.

NEMO: What did you say? I can't hear you. Say it louder.

LAYALI: Stop humiliating me.

NEMO: Just say it a little louder.

LAYALI: Fuck me.

NEMO: I'm glad that Abu-Murad's family didn't think you were good enough. I'm glad they're calling you a whore.

LAYALI: That's a mean thing to say.

NEMO: Oh, you've never been mean! And grasping. And insatiable. You would have married that motherfucker, that faggot, all because you wanted a house.

LAYALI: It's not a house I crave. It's a place free of ghosts. I can live in a shack, a box of corrugated iron that isn't fit for an animal. I could. I can even live in a tent. But, not a haunted one. Your home is haunted.

NEMO: Are you crazy?

LAYALI: It's haunted! Not even by a person, but by another house—the house your parents lost when they fled the French. I hear the ghost of that house mocking us when we can't keep the rain out. It says, "I had five bedrooms and a garden with roses of every color, suckers. You should not have left me. You should have died within my walls before you let the French take me." I never saw that house. Its ghost has no right to torment me, but it does. I want to accept reality. The French aren't going anywhere. Ever. We that work with them will profit. We that don't, don't. I can't live surrounded by ghosts. Watch your mother wear ghost gold, hear ghosts of speeches your father gave that saved the life of half of the men in our village, but not my father. But, even worse is listening to the ghost of the house they lost always laughing at us. The only way to kill the ghost of the house you had is to build a bigger one. Now, follow me deeper into the orchard.

NEMO: Why again do you want me to meet you in the orchard?

LAYALI: You're a bastard.

NEMO: Say it one more time.

LAYALI: Fine. I want you to fuck me, you motherfucking piece of shit.

NEMO: Cousin, your wish is my command

Scene 8

(Lights up on UMM *and* LAYALI. LAYALI *has her head slightly bowed.)*

LAYALI: Is it the right thing to do?

UMM: Layali, it's your life.

LAYALI: You know I'd do anything you tell me to do.

UMM: I didn't tell you to find a French boyfriend. You hate the French. I don't know why you're so keen on a being a citizen.

LAYALI: It's because I hate the French that I want to be a citizen. Because it will change what it means to be a French citizen if I am one.

UMM: But, that means you see yourself as a pollutant.

LAYALI: You're wrong. If I change what it means to be a French citizen, it will be to exalt them, not to pollute them. It will be to make it better, not worse. That's not how they see it, but they will. Or they won't. Either way. I'm going to be a citizen. What would you do in my place, Aunty?

UMM: I was born in a different time, my sweet girl.

LAYALI: My sweet girl. You haven't called me that in years. What do you advise that I do?

UMM: I advise you to do what you're doing.

LAYALI: We're not going to stay in Algeria. He's going to take me to France. Aunty, I'll be a citizen.

UMM: Just like your friend, Meriem.

LAYALI: Yes. Like Meriem.

(Lights down on LAYALI. *Lights up on* ABU, NADER, NEMO, *and* NOUNU)

UMM: I have news. Layali is getting married.

NADAR & NEMO & NOUNU: What?

UMM: Apparently, she met a man and he is interested in getting serious with her.

NOUNU: Who?

UMM: A Frenchman.

NADAR & NEMO & NOUNU: What?

ABU: The French are not our enemy.

NADER: Layali's brother is not going to allow her to marry him.

NEMO: I'm not going to allow it. Over my dead body.

UMM: Shut your mouth.

NEMO: I'll kill that French motherfucker who is trying to fuck with the women of my clan.

ABU: The French—

NADAR & NEMO & NOUNU: Enough with that, Dad!

NEMO: He's not going to marry her anyway. The French men just say that until they get what they want.

NADER: I knew something was up. I knew she had plans and they didn't include me.

NOUNU: They didn't include any of us.

UMM: He wants to enroll Layali in a beauty contest. A Miss Algiers contest!

NEMO: Miss Algiers contest! She fell for that one! Fuck this! I'm going to the whorehouse.

UMM: With what money? Don't go stealing again.

NEMO: Don't tell me what to do.

NOUNU: I made her shoes.

(Lights down on NEMO *and* NOUNU. *Lights begins to fade as* NADER *tries to exit.)*

UMM: Nader. Nader! Don't cry.

NADER: Mother. I can't take this.

UMM: Nader, she's not for you. I'll find you a better girl. A young girl. You don't care about having a wife who is younger now, but you will someday. We'll find you an only child who has some money coming to her.

NADER: I don't want anyone but Layali. She would listen to you, Mother. She would. Tell her to marry me. I don't care what she's done with the Frenchman or anyone else.

UMM: Really? *(Pause)* You're not meant to be a shoemaker and that's all you'll be if you marry her. Don't get yourself tied to a penniless girl. This writer, Jean, has offered to help you.

NADER: Jean has offered to help practically everyone, but he can't help everyone. Anyway, his infatuation with Algeria is over. He is in Lebanon now.

UMM: Then, you'll find another person to help you. Layali is too proud. And she lies.

NADER: About what?

UMM: About everything. She lies about getting postcards from Meriem in Marseille.

NADER: What? Why?

UMM: Because I told her that, once the French made all of the Jews of Algeria citizens, they won't associate with their Muslim friends anymore. She said, "No, Meriem is my best friend. Meriem said she would help me get a teaching job abroad as soon as she arrives in Marseille. Meriem this. Meriem that." I told her "Meriem will never write". It was the only thing we ever fought about. She can't bear to admit I was right. I asked the postmaster and he said he never got any mail from France for her.

NADER: That made you happy, didn't it? You never wanted her to have any friends.

UMM: That's ridiculous. Why wouldn't I want her to have friends? I just didn't want her to count on anyone and be disappointed. If she marries this Frenchman, she can be a French citizen.

NADER: She hates the French.

UMM: She'll do well in those circles. Well, as well as an Arab wife of a Frenchman can do. I know that she won't be received anywhere, but I'm not worried about her. She can help you.

NADER: No, she can help you.

UMM: I am old. I don't need help. If she gets me insulin shots or not, I'm not long for this world. I only want your happiness.

NADER: Layali worships you. If she and I were married, maybe that would change. Maybe she and I would both be closer to each other than to you.

UMM: What are you saying, Son?

NADER: I heard you telling her to marry Abu-Murad's son. What mother would do that, knowing her son loves the girl?

UMM: You think I would deliberately try to block your happiness for my own sake. Are you calling me a monster?

NADER: No, just a mother.

UMM: That's right. A mother. That girl means nothing to me compared to you. I didn't bear her into this world.

NADER: You think I can't make her happy.

UMM: No, you can't. Because she can't be happy. There are women who cannot ever be. I know, because I am one of them.

NADER: Mommy. I can't bear this.

(NADER *and* UMM *hug. Lights up on* NEMO. *Lights down on* NADER.)

NEMO: This is a fucking outrage. Our own cousin becoming a prostitute.

UMM: What are you talking about?

NEMO: He told her that he wanted to enter her into the Miss Algiers contest, right? They've been telling girls that all over Algeria. Our girls see the images of Miss France plastered everywhere and they want to be just like her. Pimps approach our girls, telling them that they know judges of beauty contests and then they rape them. After they've raped them, the girls are usually afraid to go back to their families. They become prostitutes.

UMM: That's just gossip.

NEMO: No, Mom. Wafat, one of my favorites, told me that was her story.

UMM: Who's Wafat?

NEMO: A friend. A friend that I pay to fuck.

UMM: How can you be so vulgar?

NEMO: To fuck her? Or to tell you I am fucking her?

UMM: Stop it! Stop it!

NEMO: Dad, your wife knows your niece, the daughter of Said, gets money from shady sources. Your wife likes that money, Dad, so she lets the girl work for a man famous for raping the staff. Dad, now she's selling this same stupid girl to a Frenchman, when every man in her clan wants to make her an honorable wife. Dad, you are married to a pimp.

ABU: The French are not—

NEMO: (*Grabs Father and starts choking him*) Do something! God damn it! I'm going to kill you. I'll going to kill all of you. You broke my arm, Dad. I was just a kid. It was all her idea and you broke my fucking arm.

UMM: Help! Help!

Scene 9

(*Lights up on* UMM. *The sound of sirens fading in the distance can be heard.*)

UMM: The police, as in the French police, were called and it took a lot of convincing for them not to bring Nemo in. Layali announced her engagement the next day. And, Nader…well, he didn't get out of bed for weeks. I had a bright idea that turned out not to be so bright. (To LAYALI) Bring him for coffee, Layali.

LAYALI: What?

UMM: Bring your fiancé for coffee.

LAYALI: But why?

UMM: Why not?

LAYALI: Nader won't like it.

UMM: It will help him move on.

LAYALI: How?

UMM: Seeing you with a Frenchman will make it clear that you are not the innocent little girl who grew up in this house, that you are now (Pause) changed.

(Lights up on NADER, NEMO, NOUNU, and ABU.)

NOUNU: What in the world is happening?

NADER: I can't believe this is happening.

NEMO: I can't believe I'm letting this happen.

(Lights up on LAYALI and GUN.)

UMM: Welcome, welcome! Please sit down.

NEMO: Motherfucker!

NOUNU: Is it just me or is he not normal?

NEMO: Motherfucker!

NADER: He's not normal. What is that thing on his head? He looks like a—

GUN: Bang. (Hello!)

NADAR & NEMO & NOUNU: What in the fuck?!

UMM: You drink coffee, right?

GUN: Bang. (Yes.)

LAYALI: I'll get it.

UMM: No, you sit down. How do you take your coffee?

GUN: Bang. (*Black. Thank you.*)

(*Pause*)

LAYALI: Nader, I was telling him all about your painting.

NADER: Great.

GUN: Bang. (*I'd love to see your work.*)

NADER: Excuse me? I'm having trouble understanding you.

GUN: Bang. (*I said, I'd love to see your work.*)

NADER: Excuse me for a second. Layali, can I talk to you?

(NADER *takes* LAYALI *aside to where* NOUNU *and* NEMO *are standing.*)

LAYALI: Yes? What is it?

NADER: I don't quite understand him when he speaks.

LAYALI: Oh, Nader. Your French is rusty.

NADER: My French is as good as yours. He's not speaking French. I don't hear French.

NEMO: I'm going to kick his ass.

UMM: What's wrong?

NADER: Your fiancée is talking like that to mock us, Layali. He is making gunfire sounds to mock us.

NEMO: I'm going to kick his ass.

NADER: I can't say that wouldn't be a good idea, Mom.

LAYALI: Oh, please. Stop being ridiculous.

UMM: I won't allow violence towards a guest in my house.

NEMO: Or an occupier of your country. Right. No violence. Sounds like a plan to me.

LAYALI: You don't distinguish between Arabs and Europeans when it comes to whores, Nemo. I've got to get back to him. We're being rude.

NADER: Mom understands him too. I think. Mom?

UMM: Yes?

NADER: Does the Frenchman's talk sound like gunshots when he speaks?

NOUNU: When he told you how he liked his coffee, you understood, right?

UMM: Yes, of course.

(They join GUN *and sit down.* UMM *serves him coffee.)*

UMM: Here we are. Sorry for leaving you alone like that. Layali tells me that you work in an office.

GUN: Bang. *(Yes, I work for the city. Sanitation Department.)*

UMM: My! That sounds very nice indeed.

GUN: Bang. *(Pays the bills, you know.)*

NEMO: *(Aside)* This is so fucking weird.

NOUNU: *(Aside)* What are we supposed to do?

NADER: *(Aside)* Talk to it, I guess. *(To* GUN*)* She says that you are encouraging her to compete in a Miss Algiers contest.

*(*GUN *nods his head enthusiastically.)*

GUN: Bang. *(Yes)*

NEMO: Well, it is good she is marrying a Frenchman, because an Arab man wouldn't parade a wife around like a race horse and get a kick out of other men looking at her. We think that's degrading to do to someone's daughter or sister. Degrading and disgusting.

*(*GUN *nods with a big smile, clearly not offended.)*

NADER: I guess that's what makes Frenchmen different from Arabs. Or most Arabs. But, I wouldn't have a problem with it. If I married Layali and she wanted to do anything in the world, I would let her. I would support her.

LAYALI: But, you're my cousin.

NADER: In France and England, they marry cousins too.

(Pause)

LAYALI: Mon cherie, tell them that joke!

GUN: Bang. *(Which joke?)*

LAYALI: The funny one. About Robin Hood.

GUN: Bang. *(Why did Robin Hood steal from the rich?)*

(Pause)

UMM: Why?

GUN: Bang. *(Because the poor had no money)*

(The other men watch LAYALI and UMM laugh.)

LAYALI: Ha. Get it! Because the poor have no money.

NEMO: I don't understand.

LAYALI: You see Robin Hood is a famous person who stole from the rich and gave to the poor in European folklore. So when you ask, "Why did Robin Hood steal from the rich?" the usual answer is "to give to the poor."

NEMO: No, It's not that I don't understand the joke. I don't give a shit about the joke. I don't understand him. Not a word he is saying.

UMM: Sit down, Son. *(To GUN)* Excuse us.

GUN: Bang. *(No problem).*

(GUN reaches his hand and rests it on LAYALI's knee.)

(As the exact moment that his hand touches her, NADER, NEMO, *and* NOUNU *stand up in unison, poised to fight.)*

(Lights focus on ABU. *The following lines of* ABU *should be depicted as an aside.)*

ABU: It was my choice to come to negotiate with the French.

LAYALI: Mon cherie, if you don't mind...

*(*LAYALI *slips* GUN'S *hand off of her knee.* NADER, NEMO, *and* NOUNU *step back and now play a role in* ABU'S *aside. They return to their "see no evil, hear no evil, speak no evil monkey" positions that they were in during the first scene.* LAYALI, UMM, *and* GUN *continue to sip coffee and smoke.)*

GUN: Bang. *(Is something wrong?)*

LAYALI: No, nothing's wrong. It's just my family is a bit conservative.

ABU: You call it surrender.
I call it survival.
Our children may despise us for what we are about to do.
But if I do not go and negotiate a surrender,
there will be no children left to despise us
and that is not a solution I would choose.
Hear me now, my Algerian brothers.
It is not the French who are our enemies.
I repeat, it is not the French who are our enemies.
Yes, they can colonize our land,
but not our souls.
They can torture our bodies.
But, they cannot occupy the hearts of the natives, the indigenous, the legitimate.

NADAR & NEMO & NOUNU: The dispensable.

ABU: Unless we allow it.
We will teach our children that they are Algerians
and tell them
"Your greatest weapon is the ability to think.
The weapon can be turned against you.
You can think your way into believing that, just
because someone can hurt you,
you deserve to be hurt."
So, I say, the French are not our enemies.
We are our enemies.
Our thoughts are what we must fight to the death.
Our lack of belief in our ability to keep our community
alive is our enemy.
Our lack of faith in our children to love us, even when
we are weak, is our enemy.
Our lack of hope that our roots are strong enough to
withstand anything is our enemy.
We will teach our children
the difference between being a defenseless people and
a defeated one.
That difference is knowing
that the way the world is now
is not the way the world will always be.
We should say to the French.
Come!
You, who arrived here by the power of the gun,
stay by the power of the gun,
and speak to us only in the language of the gun.
Build your cities.
But there are streets in it that will always be invisible to
you.
It is in those invisible corners that our children will
sing new anthems
to fathers who taught them
that their bodies were made for more than killing and
being killed.

NADAR & NEMO & NOUNU: The way the world is now is not the way the world will always be.

ABU: We will teach our children that they are not friendless.
All over Africa, India, and Indochina are people struggling to be free.
We will teach our children that we have friends even in the heart of Paris.
My Algerian brothers!
Tell your children,
We will not make friends easily, but we will not be friendless.
And, when your children ask you,
"Who will see the invisible?
Hear those who are silenced?
Speak for the voiceless?
Who will side with us?"
You can answer your children truthfully and say,
'The best kind of people will be our allies,
the kind who believe in justice,
the kind who understand the only way you can preserve your own humanity is by recognizing the humanity of all.
And you can tell your children,
'It will be your greatest privilege
to count such people as friends,
and your greatest responsibility to make sure you are worthy of them.'
So, if this French general and his soldiers want to force us to say a few stupid words
because they want to humiliate us, do not believe that—by making us say those words—they can humiliate us.
Said, my brother!
Listen to me.

Do not give them an excuse to kill us.
We are surrounded. There is no help coming.
Just repeat what the general has asked us to say. It
doesn't mean anything.
I've convinced the rest of the men to say it, loud and
clear, and their lives have been saved.

NADAR & NEMO & NOUNU: Half their lives.
Because they are half the men they used to be.

ABU: Half a life is better than none.

NADAR & NEMO & NOUNU: According to you. I see
things differently.

ABU: Brother, just say it. Say it, Said!

NADAR & NEMO & NOUNU: Take care of my children,
Brother. Especially my little girl.

ABU: I'm not taking care of your children. You're
taking care of your children. You're going to say it!
Don't kill him. He's stupid. Mentally retarded.
I will say it for him in his place.
There has never been a country called Algeria!

NADAR & NEMO & NOUNU: *(Overlapping!)* Long live a
free Algeria

ABU: There isn't one now, and there won't ever be!

NADAR & NEMO & NOUNU: *(Overlapping)* Long live a
free Algeria!

ABU: Shut up! Don't shoot. He doesn't mean it. I'm
going to convince him to say it. I'm going to say it for
him. I'm going to shout for him.
There has never been a country called Algeria!

NADAR & NEMO & NOUNU: *(Overlapping)* Long live a
free Algeria!

ABU: No! Don't shoot! He's my brother!

(The lights shift.)

GUN: Bang! *(Is he okay?)*

(There is a loud sound of a gunshot. ABU lurches towards GUN as if to attack him.)

ABU: No! He's my brother!

(NADER and NOUNU grab ABU before he reaches GUN. They help ABU sit down and ABU returns to his former stupor.)

LAYALI: He's a little senile. It's probably best we go.

Scene 10

(Lights up on LAYALI and GUN.)

LAYALI: Thanks for coming to meet my family.

(GUN shrugs.)

LAYALI: I'm sorry about my uncle. I've never seen him like that.

(GUN shrugs.)

LAYALI: Don't you think it would be nice if I met your parents now?

(GUN shrugs again.)

LAYALI: I mean, since we are getting married, I think it is a good idea to meet them. They'll like me. Not at first, but I can win them over. I can win anyone over. But, it doesn't matter, since we're going to live in France.

GUN: Bang. *(France?)*

LAYALI: Yes, of course. We have to live in France.

GUN: Bang. *(Why France?)*

LAYALI: What do you mean "why France?" It's very hard for Algerian wives of French husbands here.

GUN: Bang. *(I don't have a job in France)*

LAYALI: So what? You can find a job in France. There is going to be revolution in this country. My people aren't going to have your people here much longer. You're not safe here. You have to go home.

GUN: Bang. *(I was born here. This is my home).*

LAYALI: Just because you were born here doesn't make this place your home. I'm not saying such things to be rude, mon cherie. I'm saying it because I love you and want to be with you. And I want you to be safe. We should get out of Algeria. The skirmishes between our people are only going to get worse.

GUN: Bang. *(If those monkeys try anything-).*

LAYALI: Who are you calling monkeys? Your people are the monkeys. We were creating algebra while you were swinging from trees. You don't even bathe! You stink!

GUN: Bang. *(Calm down).*

LAYALI: Listen up, mon cherie. I don't think you know, but I am well-loved around here.

GUN: Bang. *(Yeah, I can tell).*

LAYALI: What's that supposed to mean?

GUN: Bang. *(The men here love you.).*

LAYALI: I don't know what you are insinuating by that. I don't mean just the men love me. The women love me too. I am the daughter of a revolutionary. A hero. Something you wouldn't understand. I gave up chances with other men. Good men to be with you. You said you wanted to marry me.

(LAYALI hits GUN.)

GUN: Bang. *(Don't hit me).*

LAYALI: Fuck you.

GUN: Bang. *(I said, don't hit me.)*

(LAYALI *continues to hit* GUN *hard.*)

GUN: Bang. (*Stop, you bitch!*)

LAYALI: First, honey, baby, sweetheart. Then, bitch.
You don't know who you're dealing with. I will get
the men of my clan to kill you if you don't honor your
promise to me. You're going to do what I say! Or
you're going to be sorry!

GUN: Bang. (*Really?*)

(GUN *pushes* LAYALI *away from him.*)

LAYALI: (*He takes a step towards her*) Stay away from me.
Stand back.

(GUN *keeps walking towards* LAYALI *and she keeps backing
away. It is the first time he should look menacing in the
play.*)

GUN: Bang. (*Or what?*)

(LAYALI *spits on* GUN.)

(GUN *raises his hand to hit her and freezes in place.* LAYALI
turns to the audience.)

LAYALI: I believed that I was incapable of being raped.
That I was untouchable. I used to go around saying
that to myself, putting myself in all sorts of situations
that women who fear rape would avoid. I realize now
that what I was recognizing was that there was a part
of me that can't be dirtied, a part of me that no one can
touch. (*Pause*) But, it is only a part.

(LAYALI *stands back in the position where she was when*
GUN *froze in place. He unfreezes and hits her. She falls to
the ground. There is a sound of a phone ringing.*)

Scene 11

(Lights up on UMM, NADER, NOUNU, *and* NEMO.*)*

UMM: Son, ignore the call.

NADER: Layali told her brother she was raped.

NOUNU: So that's what happened.

NADER: She was raped.

NEMO: She *said* she was raped. Big difference.

NOUNU: But, she was going to marry the Frenchman anyway.

NADER: What difference does that make?

NEMO: A world of difference. Between a woman who was asking for it and a woman who wasn't.

NADER: He beat her half to death, asshole!

NOUNU: Gave her two black eyes. What kind of man would give a girl two black eyes?

NEMO: Motherfucker! I've got to go join the gang of men to defend her honor!

UMM: No, son! No! One of you will die. I can't relive this.

NADER: That's a bad idea.

UMM: Right! Stay home.

NEMO: Finally, I get to kick some French ass.

NADER: I should call the police.

NEMO: Layali told her brother the neighbors did call the police, and the French motherfuckers came. But, they didn't do anything. Said the whole damn neighborhood heard what was happening—that she was screaming for help—for hours and didn't put a stop to it.

UMM: Let the other boys go! Stay safe with me.

NOUNU: Maybe she was screaming in Arabic. They didn't understand.

NADER: Or didn't care. Violence against our women is never taken care of by the French police.

NEMO: I've been waiting for this moment. Time to kick some French ass.

NADER: The French police did nothing.

UMM: That's her problem.

NOUNU: Saw she was an Arab girl.

UMM: That's her problem.

NEMO: Saw her bleeding and barely able to walk.

UMM: That's her problem.

NADER: The French police did nothing.

UMM: That's her problem!

NOUNU: I'm not a tough guy.

NADER: I should go to the salon. No one will notice I am missing.

NEMO: No choice but to fight.

NADAR & NOUNU & NEMO: That girl will be the death of me.

Scene 12

(Lights up on UMM*)*

UMM: A French police officer came to my door. He told me a group of Algerians went to the French quarter looking for a fight, looking to avenge the honor of a girl from our neighborhood, looking to say you can't harm our women without consequences. Well, actually, he told Abu, because he had been instructed that—in Arab culture—you don't address the women, but I was home and I heard him tell Abu that a son of mine had wandered off from the crowd on the beach alone and was shot by a Frenchman. For no apparent reason. I asked, "Which one?"

(Lights up on LAYALI.*)*

LAYALI: Aunty. I'm so sorry.

UMM: Which one?

LAYALI: What do you mean?

UMM: Which son died?

LAYALI: Aunty, you only have one son.

UMM: No, I have my brilliant one, Nader. My simple little one, Nounu. My bad one, Nemo. I have three sons as different in character as night is to day, day is to dusk, dusk is to dawn.

LAYALI: Aunty, you could only bear one son. You only had one son. Nader. Nounu and Nemo are our nicknames for Nader, remember?

UMM: I never loved you. I never even liked you.

LAYALI: You're in pain. I understand, Aunty.

UMM: I'm not your Aunty. I'm not your blood. You were always trying to get my attention from him, blame things on him. I bet you're glad he's dead.

LAYALI: You know that's not true. Please don't say that. Please. They're saying that they will execute the Frenchman who did this.

UMM: You little bitch! I feel nothing but hate for you. You're dead to me.

LAYALI: No. They're saying that—for once—we will get real justice.

UMM: You're dead to me.

LAYALI: I would have married Nader if you wanted me to, but you never did. You never thought I was worthy.

UMM: A woman who loved my son would not have cared whether or not I thought she was worthy. You're dead to me.

(The lights shift.)

UMM: *(To audience)* I never spoke to her again.

LAYALI: She never spoke to me again.

UMM: She went looking for a new family. She volunteered to work with the rebels.

LAYALI: I volunteered to work with the rebels.

UMM: Had I not interceded, she would have bore the great-grandchildren of the Old Storyteller of Algiers, the grandchildren of the only man who ever beat him. And me. She took on a new name. She chose to be childless, but was known as the Mother-of-All-Knowable-Knowledge.

LAYALI: Liked how that sounded.

UMM: Lightened her hair so she could pass as French. Snuck into the French quarter. Became a killer. Because she believed it was necessary to kill to create a free Algeria. She cries out at night in her sleep. I know that, not having ever spoken to her again. How do I know? Because I raised her. She used to cry at night when she was innocent, when the only violence she ever knew was the violence that was done to her.

In the ancient Arab tradition, only men were allowed to listen to the storytelling competitions. Some of the stories they heard were about women dressing as men and becoming rulers in disguise, and stories about women storytellers—one of whom told tales so captivating that she could even enchant a bloodthirsty king to listen—and therefore stop killing—for a thousand and one nights. For centuries, men told such stories to other men. In these days, though women are good enough to die and kill for Algeria, they're still somehow not good enough to tell Algeria's story. They're not good enough to even listen. Yesterday, she tried to walk in here and hear a story.

LAYALI: Yesterday, I tried to walk in here and hear a story.

UMM: You threw her out, saying women weren't allowed. It is for her sake that I told this story, left my home and came here. Infiltrated. Though I choose not to speak with her anymore—though I don't have room in my heart to feel that any comfort her presence would give me is comfort I deserve—I dislike rudeness. I am old enough that you don't dare to push me out like you did to her. Or you don't bother. Though you didn't want me here, I told my story. Though no one bet on me, I told my story. Though it's a competition and no one deigned me worthy of competing with, I told my story. And when no one wants you to tell a story and you do so anyway,

LAYALI & UMM: you automatically win.

END OF PLAY

AUTHOR'S NOTE

At the start of the Arab Spring, I was approached by
an artistic director about creating the text for a new
stage adaptation of *The Stranger*. It was a novel I had
dutifully read in high school, but had made little
impression upon me at the time. Upon revisiting it, I
realized adapting a cerebral novel wasn't my thing,
no matter how badly I wanted to work with that
particular director or needed the job. I also realized,
though I was an Arab-American kid, I missed that the
novel is about more than a weird narrator who shot
a man without feeling remorse, or a representation of
an abstract concept called Existentialism. It is about
colonist killing a native in a deeply racist environment,
where the desensitization of self and dehumanization
of others are necessary ingredients for it to survive.
Thus, the idea for this play was born. I wanted to tell
the other side of the story, evoking the wildness of the
world that was French-occupied Algeria. When two
different peoples live in one country for generations,
it can be argued that it essentially becomes a hybrid
nation. I aimed to embrace that hybridity within
the form as well as content of the story, to create
a show that encompassed Eastern and Western
live performance traditions within one theatrical
experience.

Sometimes the borders between people are figurative.
Sometime they are actual. Before I began this play,

I went to the Middle East to study the oral tradition practiced in Arab storytelling cafes, where a person could grab a cup of joe and listen to the live performances of storytellers recounting fables from *The Arabian Nights*. I chose to start my research in Syria. I naively believed it was going to remain untouched by the events of the Arab Spring and would be easy to navigate. I had travelled extensively in the Middle East and expected a smooth trip. Damascus and Aleppo were beautiful, vibrant cities. It did not seem like a place rife with revolution when I arrived. Within a week, that changed dramatically. After a quiet dinner, I left a restaurant and found myself surrounded by throngs of loud, angry, yet peaceful protestors of all ages. It felt like I had stepped into a different world. Because of the civil war, I can no longer easily access the places I was able to research on that trip, even if they do still exist. We opened our premiere of THE STRANGEST in New York in a time of travel bans on people from several Arab countries.

Skipping between two worlds as often as I do, one thing has always been clear to me. Americans who are passionate about theatre and Arabs who seek out storytelling cafes are the same in a fundamental way. They are so in love with life that they are not content to simply live their own. They hunger to experience more than they can if they stay within the confines of their own skin. Despite their differences in religion or race, they seem to belong to the same tribe in that way. Some might say that they belong to the same tribe in the only way it counts.

SPECIAL THANKS

The world premiere of THE STRANGEST was made possible in part by support from Muna and Basem Hishmeh through the Center for Arab-American Philanthropy, the Ghannam family, and the Violet Jabara Charitable Trust.

My deepest gratitude goes to Hany & Alexander Ibrahim, Dr Linda K Jacobs, Jill H Matichak, Lola Grace, Emily Morse, John Steber, Margo Jefferson, Noor Theatre, Here Arts Center, Lisa McNulty, Linda Chapman, Evren Odcikin, Mina Morita, The Field, Jose Zayas, Hanan Jaghab, Lami & Hala Taweel, Josh Zinner, Feyza Marouf, Amin El Gamal, Robin Galloway, Zahie El Kouri, Omar Fakhoury, and David Chambers. Special thanks to Sarah Leah Whitson for being a invaluable champion of this work. Much love to my parents, Charles & Ghada Shamieh.

May Adrales is an incredible director, wonderful collaborator, and brilliant theatrical mind. Thank you, May, for your wit, strength, and sharpness. American theatre would not be the same without you. In my wildest dreams, I could not have asked for a more wonderful cast who brought the first incarnation of this play to life and taught me so much. I will sing your praises until the day I can no longer sing. I am deeply indebted to the entire producing, design, and crew team. Almost all of us were strangers (no pun intended) on that first day of rehearsal, but we made magic happen. I must acknowledge the unwavering dedication of Kristen Luciani, who helped assemble an all-star team. I am particularly grateful to Allison Bressi for her extraordinary guidance, professionalism, and creativity.

Our team would like to acknowledge the support of Nadia Abu El-Haj and her staff at Columbia University's Center for Palestine Studies, who presented a staged reading at the Miller Theater in 2013. Thank you to James Schamus, who led a talkback after that reading that changed how we staged the play.

Much thanks to the Women's Project Theater, who gave us rehearsal space, coffee, and love. THE STRANGEST was workshopped as part of the Jerry A Tishman Playwrights Creativity Fund, a program of New Dramatists.

CPSIA information can be obtained
at www.ICGtesting.com
Printed in the USA
FSHW011252220120
66367FS

9 780881 457865